The Successful Coach

Become the Coach Who Creates Champions

Steve Williams

Steve Williams

© Copyright 2015 by Pinnacle Publishers, LLC - All rights reserved.

This document is geared towards providing exact and reliable information in regards to the topic and issue covered. The publication is sold with the idea that the publisher is not required to render accounting, officially permitted, or otherwise, qualified services. If advice is necessary, legal or professional, a practiced individual in the profession should be ordered.

- From a Declaration of Principles which was accepted and approved equally by a Committee of the American Bar Association and a Committee of Publishers and Associations.

In no way is it legal to reproduce, duplicate, or transmit any part of this document in either electronic means or in printed format. Recording of this publication is strictly prohibited and any storage of this document is not allowed unless with written permission from the publisher. All rights reserved.

The information provided herein is stated to be truthful and consistent, in that any liability, in terms of inattention or otherwise, by any usage or abuse of any policies, processes, or directions contained within is the solitary and utter responsibility of the recipient reader. Under no circumstances will any legal responsibility or blame be held against the publisher for any reparation, damages, or monetary loss due to the information herein, either directly or indirectly.

Respective authors own all copyrights not held by the publisher.

The Successful Coach

The information herein is offered for informational purposes solely, and is universal as so. The presentation of the information is without contract or any type of guarantee assurance.

The trademarks that are used are without any consent, and the publication of the trademark is without permission or backing by the trademark owner. All trademarks and brands within this book are for clarifying purposes only and are the owned by the owners themselves, not affiliated with this document.

Steve Williams

Contents

Introduction   v

Chapter 1: The Different Types of Coaches   1

Chapter 2 : Learning How to Motivate People   4

Chapter 3 : How to Communicate as a Coach   11

Chapter 4: Skills That Make a Great Coach   17

Chapter 5: How to Give Feedback and Critique   29

Chapter 6: Mistakes Many Coaches Make   34

Chapter 7: Building Trust and Connecting with Your Client   42

Chapter 8: Be the Inspiration   51

Conclusion   54

Related Reading   55

Stop... Before you close this book, get your free bonus...   57

Check Out My Other Books   61

Introduction

I want to thank you and congratulate you for buying the book, *The Successful Coach – Become the Coach Who Creates Champions.*

This book contains everything you will need to know to become an effective coach who is able to train and teach in a way that people will understand as efficiently as possible. Coaching is something that, at times, can be very difficult to do well. However, if done correctly, it is also something that can become very rewarding for both the coach and the trainee. There is nothing better than being able to watch others achieve something through your guidance. A great coach will not only be able to teach well, but they will also be able to create inspiration within their followers to want to better themselves and be the best they can be.

Use the knowledge you gain from this book to become a great and successful coach.

Thanks again for buying and I hope you enjoy it!

Chapter 1: The Different Types of Coaches

There was once a time that when you said the word "coach", people assumed you were talking about a sports coach but today, there are many different types of coaches. Before we get into this book I want to go over the different types of coaches and explain how this book can help each and every type.

Before we get into that, I think it is important to acknowledge how difficult it can be to be a coach. Any coach can tell you that being a coach is often a thankless job that can be frustrating and it can make you feel as if you are being judged all of the time.

For example, if you are a sports coach, every move you make in your day to day life can be scrutinized by the public. If you are a life coach, you may feel that there is no room for you to make a mistake in your own life.

When it comes to your performance at your job, it also may seem like everyone has something to say and they have plenty of tips to offer about how you could do your job better.

The good news is that no one can do your job quite like you and with the information you learn in this book, you are going to be the best coach in your field.

As we all know, there are many different types of coaches who specialize in many different areas of people's lives. Of course, there is the sports coach who helps athletes become better at a specific sport, there are business coaches, performance coaches, life coaches, relationship coaches, confidence coaches, parenting coaches, success coaches, personal development coaches, and spiritual coaches, just to name a few.

Every single one of these coaches is important to the people they are coaching and every single one of these coaches has the chance to make the person they are coaching a champion in that area of their life.

That is exactly what you are going to be learning in this book. It does not matter what type of coach you are. In each chapter of this book, you are going to learn how you can use your coaching skills to help you create champion after champion. You are going to learn how important your skills are and why there is such a high demand for them as well.

Being the very best coach you can be in your specific field not only creates champions, but also reflects highly upon you. When people are looking for a great coach in your specific field, they are going to want you to be the one coaching them, and not only that, but you are also going to be the coach others aspire to be.

Coaching is a huge responsibility and it is important that you have all of the right tools so you can be the best coach possible. A great coach knows how to communicate well without having to put someone down or belittle them. A great coach knows how to motivate the people he or she is coaching and they know how to get those they are coaching to believe in themselves.

A great coach knows their self-worth is not tied up in their coaching abilities and the success rate of those they coach. Instead, they are mentally healthy themselves and use coaching to teach life lessons to those they are coaching.

The best coaches do not make decisions for those they are coaching, but instead, try to coax the person in the right direction allowing them to make their own choices.

The Successful Coach

Those are all of the things you are going to learn throughout the rest of this book and much more.

Chapter 2 : Learning How to Motivate People

Motivation is something many people lack. They know they need to do something, sometimes it is something they want to do, not because the task is enjoyable, but because of how they will benefit from doing it.

Of course, none of this motivates people to getting the task done. If you want to be a great coach, it does not matter what type of coach you are, you have to know how to motivate people.

For example, no one wants to spend an hour a day lifting weights, but an athlete knows it is going to help them become a better athlete. No one wants to spend their entire day working on a project, but they know that is how they will pay the bills and get more clients.

It is your job to know how to motivate these people into doing things they know need to be done, that they want to get done but find no pleasure in doing. Motivation is simply the reason one has for behaving a specific way. You are the one who is going to have to help the person you are coaching find that reason.

Now there are a ton of books out there that are supposed to help people become more motivated, but trust me when I tell you, they do not work. Take it from someone who struggled with a lack of motivation for a very long time. It did not matter that I was going to be paid a large sum of money for a very small project, I lacked the motivation to get started. Why?

It was not that I did not have a reason. I wanted to get paid, it was not that I was lazy, it was not even that I did not enjoy the work, I simply had no one there to help keep me motivated.

Some people would think that the money alone should have motivated me, but studies have shown that unless there is something at stake, such as losing my house, money is not a great motivator. This is true when it comes to any reward. The majority of the time, you will find that the reward simply does not motivate people to take action.

So what are you supposed to do? Motivate people by feelings. Have you ever heard that someone was motivated by anger, fear, or even jealousy? The thing that all of these have in common is they are feelings. I am much more motivated by a feeling of accomplishment than by money.

Imagine if you were coaching a manager at a company, imagine this manager wanted to figure out how to get their employees to become more productive. Now let's say you find out that morale is low and the employees do not feel appreciated nor do they feel they are valued employees. Instead, they feel like the employer is always criticizing their work and that their jobs are in constantly in jeopardy. What would be the first thing you would do?

If you are a good coach, you would understand that the only way your client is going to get these employees to be more productive is by changing the way the employees feel. That is how your client will motivate the employee.

Now what if you are a sports coach, for example, and you have one specific team member who is simply not motivated to come to practice on a regular basis? You could, of course, threaten to cut the member from the team, humiliate them in front of the rest of their team members, or you could find out why they do not feel motivated to come to practice.

Once you find out why they do not feel motivated, you can go from there and change the way they feel. For example, maybe the person does not really feel as if they are part of the team. Maybe they feel they are not accepted as part of the team or that they do not play as well as other members of the team.

This is where you can begin to work on the emotions they are dealing with that is stopping them from feeling motivated, but first you have to really understand what the person is feeling.

You can also emphasize progress when you are trying to motivate people. One thing I personally do each day is try to do better or be better than the day before. I focus on the progress I am making and this motivates me to make more progress.

It works in much the same way as it would if someone were trying to lose weight. For example, how many times have you heard of someone giving up on a weight loss plan because they did not see the progress they thought they should see?

Either the person did not lose weight as quickly as they thought they would, they did not feel that they were increasing in stamina, or they did not think they were feeling better than they had before they started the program.

Often times, this is because people are not tracking their progress. They think they will remember how they felt, they will remember how difficult a specific task was for them; they simply think they will remember.

When it comes down to it, people do not remember so it is important for them to track their progress and for you as their coach to help them focus on the progress.

The Successful Coach

When people do not focus on how far they have come, they can easily lose sight of it and they can begin to feel like failures. This causes them to lose the motivation they have and it is your job to keep reminding them of the progress they have made so they feel motivated to continue to take the steps needed.

I remember helping a woman who was struggling with life in general. Everything was falling apart and she was unsure of where she should even begin. I decided it was best if we started with something she could see. Her house. It was a mess, she never thought she would be able to dig out from under the mess that had been created, let alone be able to clean her entire house in just a few hours.

We set a goal that each day, she would work on one specific room. When the room seemed too big for her to handle, we decided to focus on one area of that room. Each day, I had her write down what she had done and how long it had taken her.

Soon, her house was clean and in no time, she found that it did not take more than a couple hours of cleaning each day to keep it that way. Remembering how much she had accomplished was what gave her the motivation she needed when she simply did not feel like she could clean her house. That same motivation is what she uses now when taking on new projects.

Of course, depending on what area you are coaching in, you will not always be helping someone with something such as cleaning their house, but the same principle can be used no matter what area you are coaching in.

Tracking progress is important. Reminding the person you are coaching of how far they have come is extremely important and having the client spend time thinking about what they have accomplished is going to be what determines if they are successful or not.

One of the reasons people lack motivation is because a task can seem too large. I touched on this with my story, but if you want to be a successful coach and motivate people to take action, you need to be able to break the tasks down into smaller, more manageable chunks. For example, I did not simply tell the lady who needed to get her life under control that she needed to clean her house. That is, of course, what she needed to do, she needed an environment that was safe and healthy so she could live a healthy life but that would have overwhelmed her.

Instead, I broke it down into chunks. What do you think you can handle doing today? Each day, she began to realize that she was able to handle more and more. Eventually, she did not need me to ask her what she was going to do in regards to cleaning her house on a specific day. She knew she could handle it.

The truth is, as a coach, your job is to make it to where the people you are coaching do not need you any longer.

That may seem a little contradictive but when the people you are coaching no longer need you to hold their hand and walk them through every play, whether it be in a sport or in life, you have been successful at doing your job. Of course, there will be times that the person may come back to you for advice because they know they can trust you and you will steer them in the right direction but they will no longer need you to walk them through every detail.

Letting the person you are coaching know how much time it is going to take for them to get through a specific task is a great way to help motivate them. Imagine if you were running a track and the coach told you that you were going to run it until he was happy with your time. No one would be motivated except for the top runners who knew they would finish the task quickly.

There would be those on the team who felt as if they would never be done running, therefore not even feel motivated to try. Now imagine if the coach said all you had to do was run the track four times and you were finished for the night. Chances are, most people are going to run as quickly as they can so they can get the task over with and move on to something that is more enjoyable.

Another example would be if you are trying to get a child to eat their vegetables and you tell them they cannot leave the table until every vegetable has been eaten. They know they cannot do this. Instead, if you tell them they only have to eat three bites of each vegetable, they are more likely to be motivated to get it over with so they can get on with whatever it is that they want to do.

Set a limit on the tasks that are going to be perceived as painful and the person you are coaching is going to be more likely to push themselves to complete the task than if you set no limits and they have no idea how long the 'pain' will last.

Some people will tell you that rewards are a great way to motivate a person, but personally, I feel that they have the opposite effect. For example, if you are working with a factory manager who wants to get productivity up, you could tell him to reward his crew for a job well done. That sounds great and yes, productivity would jump until the reward was seen as something they were entitled to or until the reward was taken away.

If you want to reward people to motivate them, that is fine, but you have to prepare yourself for what will happen after the reward is no longer seen as a reward. If you are coaching a team, you also have to consider how the top players on the team will feel if you reward other players for doing something the top players have been doing all along.

Steve Williams

The truth is, if you want to really motivate someone to do something they perceive as painful or unenjoyable, it is your job to take the pain out of the experience and make it a pleasant one. Or you need to change the way the person thinks and feels when it comes to that specific task.

Chapter 3 : How to Communicate as a Coach

Good communication skills are key if you want to be a great coach. When we think about the word coach, we often think of someone who knows how to communicate clearly. A coach is expected to be able to easily explain what they expect, what their standards are, and how they are feeling to those they are coaching.

They are expected to be able to encourage those they are coaching and provide feedback to that person. Many people believe that a person who is able to communicate well is a person who is able to speak well as well as one who is able to use nonverbal communication such as facial expressions to communicate their thoughts and feelings.

What many people forget is that part of good communication skills is listening. This skill is often lost in many coaches, which, of course, makes the person they are coaching become frustrated because their needs, wants, and feelings are not being heard.

In this chapter, I want to focus on how you can develop good communication skills so you can not only share the way you are feeling, what you expect, your thoughts and your ideas, but so you can also understand what those you are coaching need as well.

Having good communication skills is not only imperative to your success, but also imperative to the success of those you are coaching. Not only will good communication skills help you in your coaching business, but it will also help you in other areas of your life such as your friendships or relationships.

Steve Williams

1. Body Language

There is no reason for you to be shy around the person you are speaking to. You always want to make sure your body is relaxed but that you are not slouching. If your body is tense, the person you are talking to is going to pick up on that and they are going to become tense.

When you are listening to what is being said, make sure you are looking at the person who is speaking. If you are seated, lean toward the person, and focus on what is being said.

Always make eye contact. Whether you are speaking or listening, you always want to make eye contact with the person you are trying to communicate with. If you are uncomfortable with making eye contact, look at the spot between the person's eyes and they will not know you are not looking in their eyes.

When you are listening to someone speak, nod your head occasionally, especially when the person is making a point. You do not want to get into the habit of nodding your head when you really are not listening to what is being said. This is very easy to do, but it is not how we communicate effectively. Always make sure that you are listening to what is being said and only nod when you want them to understand that you agree with their point or when you want the person who is speaking to know you have heard what they are saying.

Try your best not to cross your arms in front of you. If you are standing, you can clasp your hands in front of you, or place them behind your back or in your pockets. If you are sitting, place your hands on your lap and focus on what is being said. When you cross your arms in front of you, it can be perceived as you are closing yourself off, that you are in a bad mood, or that you are in a hurry and are not interested in listening to what is being said.

Do your best to avoid any nervous ticks you may have, such as wringing your hands. Some people pick at their fingernails or play with their hair. These are all distractions and can be perceived as a lack of interest in what is being said. If you do these types of activities, you will find that they are distracting you from what is being said.

2. **Speaking and Attentiveness**

When you are speaking, you need to be clear about what you are saying and not worry about beating around the bush. Many people are afraid to say what needs to be said, but if you want to be a great communicator and a great coach, you need to be able to speak clearly.

Always make sure you address important matters directly. You do not want to waste your time or the other person's time by telling long, drawn out stories. Often times, when you try to explain what needs to be said with a story, the person you are talking to will lose interest and their mind will begin to wander.

You need to make sure you ask if the person understands what you are trying to say to them and be willing to spend time explaining yourself if needed. Don't expect anyone to just understand what you are saying, even if it is clear to you in your own mind.

As I stated earlier, one of the most important aspects of being able to communicate well is being able to listen to what is being said. Communicating well is not only about waiting to say what you want to say. One mistake many people make is that they are not listening to what is really being said, but instead, they are thinking about what they will say next. Listen to what is being said. Repeat the point to the person who was speaking. For example: "If I understand correctly, you are saying---" Then you can take a few moments to think about what you want to say before saying it. Do not worry about the silence, it is very obvious when someone is thinking about what they want to say and it allows both parties to get their thoughts in order.

When you practice communicating this way, you will retain 75% more information than if you were to focus only on what you want to say while the other person is speaking.

3. **Consistency**

A truly great communicator is able to be consistent in their communication and is always available. You should never be afraid of someone who voices their concerns, or of having difficult conversations. You should, however, ensure that you are open to talk to those you are coaching and you need to let them know that you are able to be honest with them when you are communicating with them. Be available for those you are coaching, be bold but be tactful as well.

By doing this, you will find you avoid a lot of small issues that generally turn into larger issues because you will be known as someone who is willing to communicate at all times.

4. **Patience**

When you are communicating with others, it is always important to make sure you give them time to discuss what they are feeling as well. Only focusing on what you are trying to communicate is going to make you seem closed off and not concerned about what the other person is feeling. On the other hand, when you focus on what the other person is trying to say, it will show them you are interested in helping them with their issues.

Many people's communication skills break down at this point because they have a topic that they want to discuss and they become impatient when the other person wants to talk about something else. The fact is, you cannot control what the other person wants to or needs to talk about so the best thing you can do is to take a deep breath and listen to what the other person is saying.

If you are confused about what the other person is saying, make sure you ask questions and repeat what you are hearing back to them. Ask if you are correct about what you think they are saying. Many times, when you do this, it will allow the other person to go into depth about what they want and about their needs. This will, of course, help you understand what is going on more clearly.

5. **Follow Up**

Once someone had communicated a problem with you, your main job as a coach is to help them figure out how to handle the issue. After you have helped the person decide how they will handle the issue, it is your job to follow up with them at a later date.

This will ensure the person you are coaching knows you have listened to them and that their problems are as important to you as they are to them. This will also show the person you are coaching that you are more concerned about the bigger picture, and you want them to experience success in their lives, sport, or whatever area you are coaching them in.

When people see you are committed to them in this way, it will help them open up to you in the future and it will develop trust between the two of you.

The world today is very diverse and people communicate differently. It is because of this that it is important for you as a coach, no matter what area of life you are coaching in, to know how to communicate effectively with everyone you come into contact with.

By practicing the steps, you have learned in this chapter, you will find that more of what people are saying is sticking with you and that you are able to understand where people are coming from. You will also find that you are less likely to ask people to repeat themselves and people, not only those you are coaching, but those in all areas of your life, will have more confidence when they come to you for your help or your opinion.

It is important for you to know that great communication skills take time to learn. You are not going to learn how to be a great communicator overnight, but you will find that your communication skills are going to improve every single day.

Chapter 4: Skills That Make a Great Coach

There are many different qualities that make for a great coach, but in this chapter, I want to go over a few of these qualities as well as how you can develop these qualities so you can create champions.

The first thing I want to go over is that you have to be a great player to be a great coach. Of course, this may make you think about a sports coach, but the truth is, you have to be a great player in at least one of the areas in life, more specifically, the area you are coaching in, and you have to be able to prove it was your approach that made you great.

When you begin as a coach, people are going to look at your accomplishments in your own life and that is how they will judge your ability to coach. For example, if you are a life coach and your life is a complete disaster, you are not going to seem very credible.

The great news is, it does not matter where you're successful in life, every area can be developed and it can be used as a skill that you will coach other people in. Your approach to life is something that you can coach people on as long as it has brought you success.

It is important for you to not undervalue what you have achieved in life. Remember how far you have come and feel good about what you have accomplished. When you feel good about what you have accomplished, you will be able to help others accomplish their own goals.

One thing many people forget when they are a coach is that they stop focusing on improving their own life. They become so concerned about improving everyone else's game, they forget to work on their own. You will be judged on how you play the game, no matter what it is, always make sure that you make time to improve yourself.

You should also love what you are coaching. People change over time and you may find that you do not love the area you are coaching in any longer, but a great coach will love the thing they are coaching. For example, if you love management, then you should coach managers, if you love being an entrepreneur, you should coach entrepreneurs. Whatever it is you are coaching, you must not just be living it, but you must love it as well.

If you want to be a great coach and create champions, you have to love helping others better themselves. You should want to help others win at whatever area of life you are coaching them in. You should get great pleasure from seeing others grow and develop as well as succeed.

You cannot be the type of person who sees another person's success as competition in life. Instead, you have to be just as happy as they are when they succeed. You should take great pleasure in their triumphs.

As a great coach, you should be able to challenge those you are coaching when they are not living up to their own standards or your standards as their coach. You will have to be willing to have difficult conversations and there are going to be times when you are going to need to be tough.

However, there will also be times when you will need to be there for the person you are coaching, giving them advice and helping them as they face challenges along the way. You cannot allow yourself to get caught up in the drama of their stories. Doing so will only cause you to feel sorry for the person you are coaching and you will not feel able to push them in the right direction.

As a coach, you need to be able to step out of your comfort zone and know when you should challenge those you are coaching. Your past successes are very important, but if you want those you are coaching to thrive, what matters now is who you are coaching right now.

Being a coach means you are a leader. It is important as a coach that you understand that what you are doing is not only making a huge difference in someone's life but in the world as a whole.

A great coach does not expect themselves to be perfect all of the time. One of the biggest mistakes many coaches make is that they expect they will never fail. It is important to remind yourself, as well as those you are coaching, that you are human just like they are and you are going to make mistakes. You are going to lose your temper, you are going to have good days and you are going to have bad days. That does not mean you are not a great coach.

You should always try to learn from your mistakes, however, and hold yourself to the same standard that you would those you are coaching.

When you take on the role of a coach, you need to understand that your focus, while you are coaching, needs to be completely on the client and what they need from you. You have to put all of your attention on the client you are coaching and worry about your agenda when you are not coaching.

This can be difficult at times because we all want to become better, we want to focus on what we need to be doing at a specific time or what we want to be doing instead of on everyone else all of the time, but when you are coaching, you have to accept that your time is now their time.

One way to ensure that you are able to focus on the person you are coaching while you are coaching them is to take time out of each day to focus on you. The saying that you cannot take care of someone else unless you take care of yourself is very true. If you do not take the time to focus on your agenda and what it is that you want in your life, you will never be able to focus on helping anyone else.

Learning How to Ask Questions

When you are coaching someone, you need to be able to ask questions that are going to motivate the person you are coaching to take action. Everyone can ask a question, but there are specific ways that you need to ask questions when you are a coach.

Your questions need to be no more than seven words. You need to keep the questions short so you do not confuse the person and so you get the response that comes to their mind first. You do not want to give them a lot of time to think about what you want to hear but instead, you want an honest answer.

You should ask questions that are open ended, rather than closed. An open ended question is one that will require the person who is answering to provide you with more information whereas a closed ended question is a question that can simply be answered by a 'yes', or a 'no'. For example, an open ended question could be, "How can I help you?" whereas a closed ended question would be, "Can I help you?"

When you are asking these questions, you want to make sure you are moving the person you are coaching towards a specific goal, but allowing them to feel as if it was their idea.

For example, you can ask the person you are coaching questions like these:

1. What do you want?
2. What is important to you?

3. What do you think the first step should be?

4. What do you feel like you need to do?

5. How do you think that can be changed?

You also need to ask questions to ensure you understand what it is that the person you are coaching is in need of. If you do not understand what they are trying to tell you, simply let them know by saying something to the effect of "I'm not clear what you are saying, could you explain it again?" or "If I am hearing you correctly, you are saying..." This will ensure that there is no miscommunication with you and the person you are coaching.

If you do not understand exactly what the client is saying, but do understand some of it, you can state what you understand, then ask for help with the rest of the issue. For example:

"I understand you are having a hard time being productive during the day because you do not wake up until 10 am but I do not understand why you are staying up so late."

This will let the client know that you understand what their issue is but need a bit more explanation as to why they are dealing with this issue. If you state the question correctly, they will be able to make the correct decision instead of you telling them what it should be. In the example above, the coach did not understand why it was not important to the person they were coaching to go to bed earlier at night so they could wake up earlier and be more productive during the day.

Simply stating this will get the client to thinking about why they should be waking up earlier and it will make them decide which is more important to them, whatever they are doing at 1 am or getting a good night's rest so they can be productive the next day. Always make sure that your questions get the client to think about the decisions they need to make. This can be true if you are coaching a sports team as well, you simply need to guide the player in the right direction. With a little guidance, people often find that the answers they are looking for have been right in front of them the entire time and they will feel more confident in their decision because they will feel that they have made it themselves.

When you are coaching, try to speak with proper English as much as possible. You don't have to sound like an English teacher all of the time, especially when you are on the field or during practice, but when you are asking questions to a client or when you are sitting down communicating, you need to focus on the way you talk. Remember, even though you do want the person you are coaching to feel friendly towards you, your job is to help them and if you want to help them, you will need their respect.

Speaking with proper English is going to go a long way to make you look intelligent and it is going to ensure that your clients respect you and the guidance you are giving them.

Holding Them Accountable

A true leader, a coach who wants to see their clients or their players succeed, is going to have to hold them accountable. When you know how to hold those you are coaching accountable, you are going to get better results. You are also going to find that holding those you are coaching accountable for their actions is going to create trust in your relationship with them.

One thing you have to remember when you are holding those you are coaching accountable is that you are not responsible for their emotions. We cannot try and hold ourselves accountable for the way people react to what we have to say as long as what we are saying is not meant to cause harm or said in a mean way.

For example, imagine you are coaching a client and one of their goals is to become more productive. This example is, of course, taken from a life coach, but it would apply to any coach.

You call the client on your regularly scheduled day and find that instead of focusing on productivity, the client has been watching a lot of television and has taken up several new games on Facebook, which seems to be taking up all of their time.

It is your job to hold the client accountable. It is not your job to criticize them, but it is your job to make them understand this is not acceptable and that they are not living up to your standards nor the standards they have set for themselves.

Once you hold the client accountable, they are going to react in one of two ways. The first way is that they are going to accept accountability for their actions and they are going to be willing to move forward. The second way a client could react is in self-defense.

Now, none of this means we should not take other's feelings into consideration when we are speaking and as a coach, it is very important for you to know the person you are talking to. What this does mean, however, is that you do not have control over how someone reacts to you.

To know how to handle a defensive person, you have to first understand why they have become so defensive. We will assume for the sake of this book that your tone of voice or the way you spoke to them had nothing to do with them becoming defensive.

Many people become defensive because they are afraid of change. It does not matter that they know the change is going to cause them to benefit in life, it is natural for people to fight against change and it is natural for them to go on the defense when doing so.

Another reason people may become defensive is because they want to maintain an illusion they have. This could mean that even though they know they did not get everything they wanted to get done in a specific time frame, they make themselves believe it was not their fault. This happens a lot when people get distracted by television or the Internet.

Many people find that they feel they are busy when they are online, but when it comes down to it, they are not being productive at all. This is especially true for entrepreneurs and for those who work on a computer all day long. People want to believe they are doing everything within their power to make positive changes in their life and they don't want anyone else telling them otherwise.

Finally, people become defensive when they think what you are suggesting is going to have a negative impact on their life, their self-confidence, or the way they feel about their life.

When you are dealing with a person who becomes defensive, you need to be able to feel empathy for them and you need to be able to understand where they are coming from.

It is your job as the coach to figure out if the person you are coaching is afraid of failing and therefore never really tries, if they are simply being lazy and wasting your time as well as their own, or if they perceive the changes that are being made as a threat to the way they think about their own lives.

You need to allow yourself to understand how emotionally taxing the change is for the person you are coaching and understand that when they become defensive, it is simply their way of saying they are afraid of what might happen if they do make the changes.

If the person you are coaching thinks you are attacking them for not taking the steps they were supposed to take, chances are, they are not going to be willing to listen to any of the suggestions you have. If this is the case, you can ask them to tell you about their experiences with change, ask them what changes they think they can make in their life that would be beneficial and allow them to tell you why making changes in their life is so difficult for them.

You do not have to agree with everything the person you are coaching has to say, it does not have to seem rational to you nor does it have to make any sense at all, but you need to be open minded and try to understand where they are coming from.

When you begin opening yourself up to the way your client is thinking, they are going to begin to trust you and see that you are not out to cause them harm but are instead there to help them. They will also see that you think highly of them and want them to be happy throughout the entire coaching process.

Become Encouraging and Supportive

Being supportive is a very important quality for a coach, but you don't want to overdo it. Of course, you should be your client's cheerleader, but you don't want to fake the enthusiasm or your client will see right through you.

To be supportive, you need to be an active listener. Of course, being an active listener has come up several times in this book, but I cannot stress how important it is. If you do not listen to what the person you are coaching is saying, it can make them feel as if they are unimportant, that they are nothing more than a paycheck. Instead, try and show empathy. Let them know that you understand they are struggling and that you are there to help them.

The next step of being supportive is to offer constructive feedback. When your client is looking to you for support or advice, you should avoid judging their actions or speaking too harshly to them. This could cause them to shut down and be less likely to talk about what they are dealing with in the future. You need to remember that although something may seem simple to you, it can seem very complex to the client.

Instead of telling the person you are coaching that they should behave a specific way or choose to follow a certain path, ask them if they have considered a specific perspective or ask your client to put themselves in another person's shoes. Try to prompt the person you are coaching to think more critically about what they are experiencing and be there to listen to what they are feeling.

The third step to being supportive is being available to the person you are coaching. You need to recognize that the person you are coaching may be scared or confused about what they are going through. They may have had to deal with devastation in their lives and they may be trying to overcome the pain that came with it. Let the person know that no matter what they are going through, you are there to help them through it.

Finally, turn into the client's cheerleader. You need to understand that you may be the only person in the client's life who is supporting the changes they are trying to make. Being positive and validating the client's feelings while focusing on the bright side is going to help your client feel better about their strengths, accomplishments, and progress. You should always be sure to point out how proud you are for the accomplishments and progress they have made.

The last thing I want to cover in this chapter is how to encourage those you are coaching. Being a coach is more than just smacking someone on the butt and telling them 'good job'. To encourage your clients, make sure you:

1. Learn how the person speaks. This does not mean how they say the words that come out of their mouth, but how they speak encouragement to others. Not everyone is going to feel encouraged in the same way and one of the ways you can learn how people prefer to be encouraged is by the way they encourage others.

2. If you have an encouraging thought about a specific person, share it with them. When you are speaking to the person you are coaching make sure you tell them when you are proud of them for what they have accomplished.

3. When a person is dealing with a specific problem, help them find a specific answer. Ask them what they feel like their next step should be and encourage them to follow through with it.

4. Always recognize even the smallest efforts. You may expect the person you are coaching to reach specific goals, but there are going to be times that the goal is just not met. However, this is not the time for you to make the person you are coaching feel bad about not meeting their goals, instead, let them know that you are glad they are making progress toward their goals and that you are proud of them for doing so.

5. Do not focus on what is being done wrong, but instead, focus on what is being done right.

6. Do not allow the person you are coaching to speak poorly about themselves. When you have a client who puts themselves down, stop them and give them a compliment instead. However, if you feel they are fishing for compliments, figure out why.

7. Don't try to flatter the people you are coaching. People know the truth about themselves, they know when another person is trying to flatter them. This makes them not trust the person who is flattering them. Instead, be honest and try to put a positive spin on what they are doing.

Being a coach is a huge responsibility and it takes a lot of skills but the good news is, you can improve upon any of these skills and the more you improve, the better experience the person you are coaching will have. By using these skills, you will be able to create a champion!

Chapter 5: How to Give Feedback and Critique

The first thing you need to remember when you are giving feedback is that it needs to be constructive. This is something a lot of people forget and it can lead to a lot of problems in life. When you are giving feedback to someone you are coaching, you want to make sure you are being constructive.

Your feedback needs to be based on the information you have, focused on the issue, and based on what you have observed. There are two different types of feedback you can give: praise and criticism. Both of these are personal judgements about the performance, effort, or the outcome of something the person you are coaching had attempted. Of course, praise is used to convey a favorable judgment and criticism is how we convey an unfavorable judgement.

The information you will provide will be general and it will be focused on the person you are coaching, it should be based on your opinions and feelings but also on what the client wants to achieve.

When you are giving feedback, you should always be direct. Make sure you get straight to the point instead of beating around the bush. It can be difficult to give negative feedback, but it is much easier to do so if you simply get to the point.

Avoid telling the person you are coaching that they 'need to', this implies they are not doing what they should be doing and you know how to do it better. For example, "Jane, you need to start waking up earlier if you want to get anything done during the day." This is not really providing any feedback, but is instead telling the person you are coaching what you think they should do. It implies that the person is not trying. Instead, try to clarify your feedback. For example, "I am disappointed that we agreed you would get up at 8 am and you are still sleeping until 10 am. What do you think can be done to make the changes that need to be made?"

Be sincere when you are giving feedback and always try to avoid sending mixed messages to the person you are coaching. When you are sincere, it shows not only that you respect the person you are coaching, but that you care about them as well. Mixed messages usually contain a 'but'. For example, "Jane, you have done well, but..." This tells the person you are coaching that they have done a great job but it was not good enough. One thing many people believe is that when there is a 'but' in a sentence, you can't believe anything before that point.

Always express appreciation and when you have to give negative feedback, do so by expressing concern. It is important to ensure that you do not use tones such as frustration, disappointment, anger, or even sarcasm when you are giving negative feedback. Instead, use a tone of concern to show you do care about what the person is going through and to create a sense of caring.

It is important to remember that the entire purpose of negative feedback is to create an awareness about the performance or behaviors so the performance or behaviors can be improved in the future. If you provide feedback in a helpful manner, you will ensure the person you are coaching is able to accept the feedback. If, however, you cannot provide the feedback in a way that will help the person you are coaching, you will defeat the purpose of providing feedback.

You need to remember that it is important to provide feedback while talking to the person physically. It is best to provide feedback when you are speaking to a person face-to-face, but, of course, that is not always possible. If it is not possible for you to see the person you are coaching face-to-face, you can speak to them over the phone and provide the feedback. Never use email, messaging, or texts to provide feedback.

The reason for this is because the tone of voice means everything when you are providing feedback. When you send an email or a text message, there is no tone of voice to be heard and it is up to the person reading the message to decide what tone of voice is being used. This means that even if you mean to say something in a caring voice, it can be taken as a sarcastic tone. Never leave it to someone to interpret how you mean to say things. Instead, make sure they hear it out of your own mouth, just how you want them to hear it.

Before you provide feedback, you need to have a plan. The first thing you need to know is what you are going to say. What is going to be the content of the feedback?

The first sentence you say should identify the issue you will be discussing. What topic is the feedback about? This should be followed by specific occurrences you know have happened. Begin each point with 'I'. For example, "I have noticed", "I have seen", and so forth.

You should focus on timing as well. You should give feedback in real-time as much as possible. Do not let someone you are coaching continue a behavior that you need to discuss for a long period of time because they will feel that there is nothing wrong with it and you will completely take them off guard.

Here is an example:

You are coaching Mary; she is an entrepreneur and has asked you to coach her. Mary is struggling with focusing on her business and is easily distracted, oftentimes, not completing the work she is supposed to on any given day.

If you do not express concern about this type of behavior and provide the proper feedback immediately, Mary is not going to understand why, after two months of displaying this behavior, you finally say something.

It is also important to give positive feedback in real-time. For example, if Mary has a great week and focuses on her work with minimal distractions, you need to be able to provide feedback for this as well. Doing so will motivate her to perform even better the following week.

The final question would be: "How often do I need to provide feedback?"

The answer to this question is: Every time you speak to the person you are coaching. It does not matter if you speak to the person twice a week, three times a week, or once a month. After the person has informed you of the progress made, or the lack of progress, you need to provide feedback so the person you are coaching has direction.

When you provide feedback, you are allowing the person you are coaching to look at what they are doing and decide if it is in their best interest to continue in that manner or if they should focus on improving.

You need to make sure that you provide a lot of detail for the person you are coaching. You can do this by describing the situation as you see it, but you need to do so in a constructive manner.

For example, you do not want to simply tell a person you are coaching that you think they are just being lazy and that they need to suck it up. Instead, you should break it down for them. Find out why they are not getting things done that they need to get done. Ask them why they are not meeting their goals and find out why they do not feel it is important to focus on their goals.

I have heard many coaches get angry with the people they are coaching, telling them that they are wasting their time and their money. They get loud and the truth is, this is only costing that coach business and it is not helping the people they are coaching at all. Your job as a coach is to motivate and encourage the person to move toward their goals.

If you have set a specific goal and the person you are coaching and they have not attempted to reach that goal, it is important that you are straightforward with them and express what you are observing. Ask the client if they understood the goal and if they agree with it or if they think there should be changes made. Make sure you reach a mutual understanding about what is expected by both you and the client.

Finally, you will need to develop a plan with the client or the person you are coaching that will ensure their success. You will not develop this plan yourself, but will develop it with the client's input.

Chapter 6: Mistakes Many Coaches Make

No coach is ever going to be perfect and mistakes are going to be made, but I feel it is important for you to understand the most common mistakes coaches make so you can avoid them and focus on your client's success.

Many coaches make the mistake of trying to change too much too quickly. When you start a new program with a new client, it is important for you to provide stability for them. Although you will not want to make a lot of changes all at once, you will want to set expectations and implement practices that will ensure your client's success.

It is important that you don't try and change too much all at once because as we discussed earlier, it is natural for people to fight against change. It can also be very overwhelming for the person you are coaching if they are trying to implement a lot of change all at once.

Instead, choose which area is the most important and start making small changes in that area.

The second common mistake many coaches make is to allow the person you are coaching or even the parents of the people you are coaching to have too much control over you as a coach.

If you are coaching a team of children, it is important to allow parents to express what they feel should happen on the team as well as with their children. It is also important for there to be a balance between what the parents or the client (for those who are not coaching a child's sports team) want and what you know is best as a coach. Hear what your client is saying, respect what is being said, and be available to listen, but always make your own decisions.

The Successful Coach

You are the coach and it is important for you to make that clear.

The third issue many coaches face is lack of organization. This is especially true for coaches who are working with several clients at the same time. It is important for you to know exactly where your planner is; it is important for you to know who you are meeting with, when you are meeting with them, and what you will discuss. If you are coaching a team, it is important for your binder to be organized with the information you will need on each player on the team such as contact information as well as health information.

Lack of communication is another issue many coaches face and that causes many issues when they are coaching. It is important for you to communicate with those who are on your team or who you are coaching. You want to set clear expectations in the beginning and make sure the person or people you are coaching understand what is expected of them. Make sure you communicate clearly and allow those you are coaching to ask questions. One thing you can do is have the person you are coaching or the players and the parents sign a paper stating that they understand what your expectations are before you start coaching.

It is also important for you to set boundaries with those you are coaching. It is very easy for you to have no boundaries when you are a coach, no matter who you are coaching or the age of the person you are coaching. Regardless of the age of the people you are coaching, or what you are coaching them for, it is important to remember that they look up to you and you need to behave in a professional manner.

It is very easy for a coach to feel as if they are friends with those they are coaching and to become more involved in their life than they really should be. It is also very easy to begin feeling comfortable around those you are coaching and to forget that you need to behave like a professional.

This is a common mistake and it is important for you to ensure that this does not happen. You also need to ensure that your clients or those you are coaching treat you as a professional and explain to them that there will be a zero-tolerance policy if they do not treat you like a professional.

The next mistake is some coaches forget to work on themselves. It is very easy to become so caught up in helping those you are coaching that you forget to focus on yourself but this is extremely important. You should not be spending all of your time focusing on improving the lives of those you are coaching, but spend time focusing on improving your life as well. When you see success in your life, you will be able to teach those you are coaching how to reach that same level of success.

Many coaches do not give it their all. Now this is not to say that you should give every ounce of energy you have every single day to coaching; we know that this is not going to do anyone any good and is going to do more damage than it is good. What it is saying is that you cannot be a coach if it is something you are only going to do halfheartedly. You need to be willing to do what it takes to be successful and to ensure the success of your clients or those you are coaching.

Working with family or friends is a big no-no for the most part. If you are coaching the little league team, that is one thing, but if you are a life coach or any other type of coach, besides a sports coach, it is usually best not to coach family or friends.

Even as a sports coach, you will find that there are problems that arise when you coach friends and family. One of these issues could be that your friends and family expect special treatment, no matter how well they play.

The Successful Coach

When it comes to other types of coaching, it is important for the coach to come in with no opinion of the person, in other words, the coach needs to have a blank sheet that will allow them to focus on what the client needs.

When you coach a family member or friend, you will already have a large amount of knowledge about that person. Some of the knowledge will be correct and some of it will not be and chances are, you will have an agenda of your own, which will take your focus away from the agenda of the person you are coaching.

Many coaches are also afraid of silence; they are always in a hurry to fill the void. The truth is, you need to become very comfortable with silence in a coaching session because it can be very beneficial. You have to understand that people will always rush to fill the void of silence when we are talking to someone we do not know well. If you have ever been on a date, you will understand what I am talking about.

People would rather talk about anything than have that awkward silence. Oftentimes, it will begin with talking about the weather, or even what the person does for a living, but it is a starting point for conversations that will lead to more informative conversations.

When you ask a question, you need to remain silent until the client or the person you are coaching answers you. The long pause means they are thinking about what you have asked and trying to figure out what the best answer is. Silence is usually a very good thing when you are working in the coaching world.

You also need to remember that not all people think in the same way as you do and they do not process information in the same way as you do. If you do not understand that other people do not think the same way you do, you will be reducing the effectiveness of your coaching process.

When someone tells me that another person did not understand them, the first thing I think is that it would be strange if they did. We have to remember that no one is going to understand what we are thinking or saying 100%, no matter how much we try to explain it.

When a client or a coach do not understand that others do not think the same way they do, they have to deal with a lot of frustration in life, especially when they do not get what they want and they often fall into the victim mindset.

Many people, not only coaches, forget that they need to expose themselves to new information and viewpoints. Oftentimes, people believe the way they believe and think the way they think because it was what they were taught growing up. They do not form an opinion for themselves. There are times, however, that when they are exposed to new viewpoints and new information, they begin to form their own views.

As a coach, you need to understand that your client or the person you are coaching can suffer from confirmation bias, this often leads to their progress being hindered because instead of focusing on the changes that need to be made, they are focusing on finding the evidence they need to back up what they believe.

For example, they may refuse to take part in meditation because they feel that it is against their religion or that it is some form of devil worship. None of this is based on fact, but they are not going to focus on the benefits of meditation because they are going to be too busy defending what they have been taught.

Assuming that you know what the client is talking about is another huge mistake many coaches make. Take this conversation, for example:

Coach: You seem a bit upset today, is there something you would like to talk about?

Client: I am so sick of it. I hate him.

Now imagine that you had just talked to another client who was having problems in her marriage. Chances are, you are going to assume that the client is having problems with their husband.

You may think that she found out he is cheating again, or that she is ready to leave him.

The truth is, you have no idea what is going on or who she is talking about. Instead of assuming you know what is going on, you need to start asking questions so you do not find yourself wasting time, and setting off down the wrong path when trying to help the client.

What is worse than wasting time is the fact that you will look unprofessional and foolish trying to help a client find a solution in an area of their life where there really is no issue in the first place. Instead, make sure you ask plenty of questions and really know what is going on before you make assumptions and begin giving advice.

There are times when coaches focus far too much on winning. You have to remember, no matter what area of life you are coaching in, it is not all about winning. When you are coaching a sports team, it is about learning how to interact with others, work as a team, and have fun. When you are coaching in other areas of life, it is about learning from experience, and improving yourself and your life.

Of course, winning does matter to an extent. It does feel great to win games, it does feel great to win at life, but it is not about winning, it is about the process. When a coach focuses too much on winning, they take the joy of the process away and often times, life lessons are not learned when they should be. You should never take on the attitude "Win, no matter what the cost."

One very common mistake many coaches make throughout all areas is that they do not understand that not everyone can be coached in the same manner. People learn differently, they have to be approached differently, and they have to be coached differently. This means coaches have to learn different ways of coaching.

What typically happens is coaches get stuck in a rut when it comes to coaching. They find that one specific way of coaching works really well for a few specific people and they expect it to work for everyone. This is never going to happen. The way you coach has to change with the people you are coaching.

Ineffective use of time is another common problem many coaches face. It is not only the baseball coach who finds himself hanging out and talking to the team instead of practicing but it is all coaches who suffer from this issue. You need to remember that you only have a specific amount of time with those you are coaching each week and you need to use that time as efficiently as possible.

Interrupting a client when they are speaking as a way to save time is a huge mistake. You need to remember that many times, the only safe space a client has to open up is when they are speaking to you. Some coaches do not feel that it benefits the clients when they spend a lot of time focused on one particular issue or problem they are dealing with in their lives, but it is very important for your client to be able to empty their feelings out. The process of emptying their feelings out often takes that power of the feelings away and puts the client back in control of their own lives. You need to remember that many times, clients do not have a lot of people who they can talk to or open up to. Be one of the people they can open up to.

The Successful Coach

A lot of coaches make the mistake of talking far too much. Instead, you need to remember that you should only be speaking 20% of the time and you should spend the other 80% of your time with your client listening. Your job as a coach is to listen to what your client has to say without judging them and without an agenda of your own. Many coaches feel they need to give advice when, in reality, the client simply needs to be heard. It is important for your client to know that they will not face judgement when they are talking to you and the best way to ensure they know this is to listen to what they have to say.

Everyone wants to fix people's problems, but when you are a coach, you have to remember to get that fixer inside of you under control. It is not your job to fix your client's problems. The truth is, the answers have to come from the client even if we as coaches think we know what is best for the client. Remember, change is difficult, but change is not going to stick if it does not come from the client.

Chapter 7: Building Trust and Connecting with Your Client

When you are a coach, you need to know how to build rapport with a client. Rapport is defined as a relationship between two people that is based on a mutual understanding as well as trust.

When you are a coach, rapport is the connection that you as a coach and your client or the people you are coaching establish while you are working together. It is the trust that your client or those you are coaching has for you.

Think about the way you feel about a doctor, dentist, or other professional. You may not personally know the person, but you have established a rapport with them. There is a mutual understanding and a trust. You had this same mutual understanding and trust for teachers when you were in school as well as many other people in your life.

Building rapport is very important when it comes to the success of a coach/client relationship because it promotes communication, it helps to develop trust, and it fosters as desire in the client to participate in the program you have set out for them. Without rapport, the coach/client relationship cannot flourish and the client or person you are coaching will not be as successful as they would be if they trusted you.

For some people, it is very easy to build rapport; it seems to come naturally to them. These people are often very warm and welcoming type of people, they are genuinely interested in getting to know those they are coaching and they want to help them.

Others have to learn this skill and there are many programs available that will teach you how to build rapport. You can build rapport through open communication with those you are coaching and by sharing positive experiences. It really is no different than if you were to build a relationship with anyone else. You have to gain your clients' trust, they have to know that you are there for them and that you care about their success.

You have to remember that your clients need to have confidence in you. They are going to be opening up to you and talking to you about issues they probably will not open up to anyone else about. They need to understand that you are not going to judge them and what they say is going to stay confidential.

It is very important for you to remember that the way you interact with the people you are coaching during the first few sessions is going to set the tone for the entire relationship.

The good news is that many coaches are very good at building rapport but there are those who simply lack the skills to do so.

I want to share a story with you about a coach I once knew. This coach was a highly educated man and because of that, many people recommended him. We will call him Dave for now.

Dave was a local coach who went to his clients' homes once a week for about an hour. I immediately began to see problems with the way Dave interacted with his clients while watching him. One of the first things I noticed was that Dave was rarely on time for the appointments, often missing the scheduled appointment and showing up at the client's house whenever he deemed fit.

Steve Williams

There were times when he would miss an appointment, then show up to a client's home when they were not home, simply leaving a note on the door stating that he was there. This, of course, upset many clients, especially when this happened on the very first appointment.

The second thing that stood out to me was how much time Dave spent talking about himself when he was at a client's house, how much time he spent talking about other clients and how little time he actually talked to the client about their own issues. After speaking to several clients, I found that they thought he was arrogant and only wanted to talk about himself.

The truth was that Dave was not arrogant at all but he was trying to build rapport with the client by keeping things casual, by acting like he was their friend. In reality, he was losing a lot of respect and would have been much better off to act professionally.

The point of this story is to remind you that when you are in doubt, behave like a professional to build rapport. Keep your appointments, never talk about what is going on with other clients, and don't get caught bragging about how great your life is or how much you know. This is going to make you lose clients and is going to make people become very annoyed with you.

Of course, this is how some people make friends so if this behavior sounds familiar to you, please remember that it does not work when you are building rapport in a business relationship.

You want to make the people you are coaching feel as if they have just met a new friend, or that they have known you much longer than they really have. They have to know that you are going to understand the issues they are dealing with.

The Successful Coach

This was one of Dave's issues. This was a married man who had retired from the Navy, went to college twice, and had more money than he knew what to do with. Yet he was coaching single mothers. When these women looked at him and listened to his stories, they did not feel a connection with him because they did not think he understood where they were coming from.

It does not matter if you have been in the specific situation the person you are coaching has found themselves in, what matters is that you need to make them think you understand the problem and that you are the person who will help them reach their goals.

It is also important to understand that when it comes to a coaching client, you usually only have one chance to make a good impression. If you do not start building rapport on the first meeting, chances are, the client is not going to want to work with you and will find another coach instead. If you are coaching a team and you do not begin building rapport right away, chances are, you are going to watch your entire team fall apart.

To finish up this chapter, I want to give you some tips on how you can build rapport.

1. Be yourself. No matter what type of relationship you are building, every professional will tell you that you need to be yourself. Do not be a chameleon.

2. Be predictable. There are many people who desire spontaneity in their lives, but the strongest relationships are built on predictability. It does not matter how boring it sounds, be the coach people can come to and know how you will react to what they have to tell you. Be the coach they know will be there for them.

3. Always keep the promises you make. If you make a promise to one of your clients, to your team, or to the people you are coaching, make sure you keep it. If you say you will do something, make sure you do it. This will show that your word is good and you are a trustworthy person.

4. Admit when you have failed. It is important to remind those you are coaching that you are human and that you do make mistakes. By admitting you have failed, you are setting an example for those you are coaching. Do not blame your failures on anyone else but take responsibility for them and show those you are coaching that failure is not the end of the world.

5. Always make sure that you answer your texts, emails, or return phone calls in a timely manner. If you receive a message from a client or a person you are coaching, it is important that you do not put answering the message off until it is convenient for you. Of course, there are going to be times when you are going to need to wait to answer a message or to return a call, but always make sure you do so as soon as possible.

6. Set boundaries from the beginning. Make it clear to those you are coaching that when you are with your family, you are not available for calls. Explain when you can speak to them and what your boundaries are when it comes to what you can talk about.

Imagine what your deal breakers would be, what would it take for you to stop coaching this specific client or team? Make sure they know those boundaries.

7. Openly talk about your doubts. Oftentimes, people will think they can accomplish more than what they really can. The truth is, people expect to get 30% more done in any given time period than is humanly possible. If you find that the person you are coaching believes they will be able to complete more than you think they can, let them know about those doubts and explain to them why you feel this way. Make sure you have a good reason and do not make the client feel as if you simply do not believe in them.

8. Discuss commitment with your client or the people you are coaching. Explain to them that the program they are taking part in is going to take time and commitment and that you need to know that they are willing to give that. Let's be honest, if the person or people you are coaching are not willing to commit to the program, they are wasting their time as well as yours. If they are not willing to commit, you can move on to helping someone who is willing to commit. If they are willing to commit, hold them to it.

9. Understand that there are going to be bumps in the road. There are going to be times when the person or people you are coaching struggle to focus on what you need them to do. There are going to be

times when they feel like giving up and there are going to be times when you feel like giving up as well. It is important for you to communicate with the person you are coaching and to support them when they are having a hard time.

10. Make sure you clearly state what you expect. When the person you are coaching knows exactly what you expect of them, they are more likely to try and achieve it than if they were playing a guessing game, hoping that what they are doing is what you expect.

11. Do not gossip, do not talk about other clients, or other people you are coaching. Do not share a person's problems with other people. It is fine for you to talk to another coach about how you can help a specific person if the other coach has no idea who you are talking about. Never talk to other clients about a different client.

12. Keep the secrets that are told to you. This can be very hard for some people. There are some things that are so interesting that you just want to talk about them. If you are told a secret, and the client or the person you are coaching is not in harm's way because of the secret, keep it to yourself.

13. Don't be late and don't miss appointments. We are all busy. We all have things we need to get done every single day. When you are late for an appointment with those you are coaching, it shows

them that they are not important to you, and they will not trust you to keep your word in the future. Being on time shows that you respect the person you are meeting with and that you understand they have other things to do.

14. Always try to understand first where the client or the person you are coaching is coming from then focus on being understood yourself.

15. Never lie. If you do not think your client is taking the best course for them, do not lie and say that you agree with them. They will respect you much more if you simply tell the truth and back it up with facts.

16. Learn how to accept criticism. You are going to be giving both positive and negative feedback to those you are coaching, but are you able to accept both positive and negative feedback? Many people feel crushed when they are given negative feedback and they allow it to stop them in their tracks. Instead, listen to the feedback, make the changes you can make, and then learn from the experience.

17. Make people feel that they matter. Don't be fake and over the top, but make sure your clients understand that they do matter to you and that you are a coach for a reason, that the reason has nothing to do with a paycheck.

18. Focus on your own reputation. If you are a coach, people are going to be watching you all of the time. Open the door for the lady at the grocery store. Smile and say hi to someone who looks as if they are having a bad day. Be a pleasant person and build a strong reputation.

19. Go above and beyond what is expected of you. Many people do just enough to get by. They want to get the job done and that is their entire focus but you should be going above and beyond that. Send out an email to the people you are coaching, simply checking on them and making sure they are doing okay. Send out birthday presents, remember important dates, and make them feel important.

20. Learn how to trust others. If you do not trust others, no one is going to be able to trust you. Spend time every day, making a habit of trusting other people.

When you make each one of these tips a habit, you will find that it is very easy for you to create rapport with your clients or the people you are coaching. You will be seen as trustworthy and be given trust by those you interact with on a regular basis as well as by those you are just starting to work with.

Chapter 8: Be the Inspiration

I started this book out by teaching you how to motivate people. Although there are many different ways to motivate those you are coaching, and it is all dependent upon the person you are coaching, inspiring people is much easier.

Think about the person who inspired you. At some point in your life, there was someone who made you want to be a better person. They made you want to become successful and they helped set you on the course that led you to where you are even if they did not know it.

Part of my job and my responsibility as a person is to inspire those around me. It is important to understand that you cannot control how or if you inspire anyone. Inspiration is a feeling that comes from deep within. It is the ability to look at someone, see what they are doing, and have it resonate deep within you while feeling motivated to become like what has inspired you.

By definition, inspiration is that act of inhaling or taking in. I like to think of it as the taking in of motivation to become better at a specific aspect in life.

Part of what I do is to inspire people to better their lives, to show them through my own life that they can have the life they want, that they do not have to depend on others to give them what they need and that their dreams can come true.

The great thing about this is when I bring someone into my life who feels as if they have hit rock bottom, when I show them how far I have come in my life and that they can do it, too, it inspires me to work even harder and to reach other people while it is motivating them to take action in their life.

Steve Williams

How can you inspire people? The first thing you have to do is leave your ego at the door. If I walked around with a chip on my shoulder about how far I have come in life, I would not inspire anyone to follow in my footsteps. Instead, you need to remember that, at one point, you did not have it all together, you had to learn just like those you are coaching had to learn and it is great if you can share your story with those you are coaching.

You do not need to brag about what you have done, how far you have come, or what you have. Let your actions speak for themselves, let your life speak for itself, and focus on being the best person and coach you can be.

Show the person or people you are coaching what winning looks like. You need to let the people you are coaching know what the end state looks like. Then you can talk to them about how they will get there. Many people will try to simplify this and tell people that the shortest distance between two points is a straight line and although this is true, this is not how lives are changed nor how goals are met. Let the person you are coaching know that they are going to be making many zig zags along the way and that it is perfectly okay to do so.

Use the talent you have to inspire those around you. I am a very factual based person. Before I take on any task, I have to do a lot of research and know exactly what I should expect. Many people do not have the ability to sit down and research specific issues and they do not have the ability to map out a plan. This is where I come in. I use my talent to break their goals down for them into manageable portions and show them what is going to occur when they follow through with the plan we have made. In just the same way I do, you can use your talents to help those you are coaching. Of course, not all of us have the same talents and that is why using your talent is a great way to inspire people. It can even inspire them to search for what their own talents are.

Speak up. Let those you are coaching know how you feel about a specific topic, let them know that they have the ability to speak up about how they feel and what they believe in. When you allow them to voice the way they feel with you, they will become inspired and begin allowing their voice to be heard elsewhere.

The truth is, the only way for you to truly inspire people is to live a life that is true to who you are. For me, that means I am a strong and dependable person who loves to help those around me. For someone else, it is going to mean something completely different. What you will find is that you will inspire those who are likeminded. Those who are going through what you have gone through in the past are going to be inspired by you.

Be the air that people inhale, be the inspiration those you are coaching need and you will find that you are creating champions everywhere you turn.

Conclusion

Becoming a successful coach can not only be very profitable, but it is very satisfying as well. I hope this book was able to shed some light on the different ways of thinking that lead to successful coaching as well as provide a good resource of techniques and strategies to coach effectively. It's not always going to be an easy task, however, you can greatly improve your coaching skills by taking what you've learned and applying it to your own life. The possibilities are endless as long as you stay determined and never give up!

I hope this book was able to teach you how to become the coach who creates champions.

Thank you again for buying this book!

Steve Williams

Related Reading

I have the perfect complement to this book on coaching to help further you in your career and coaching goals. Learning how to coach is more than simply being a coach. You must become a great leader. For some this may come naturally, however, for others it takes a lot of practice and hard work. Maximizing your leadership potential will simultaneously maximize your effectiveness as a coach.

I highly recommend that you check out my book, ***The Successful Leader – Maximize Your Potential and Lead Like You Were Born to!*** It is available on Amazon in paperback and digital format.

Steve Williams

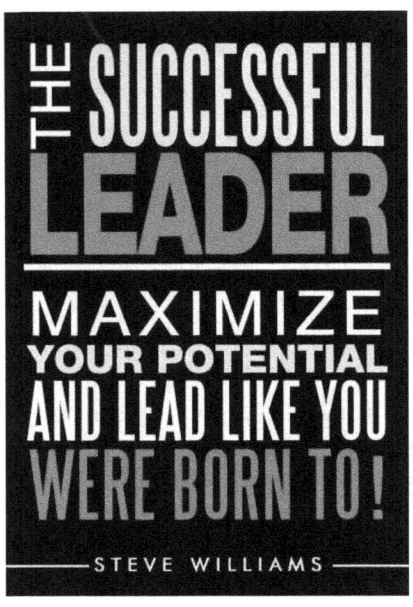

Scan The Above Code or Go Here to View on Amazon:
http://www.amazon.com/dp/B017TBSK18/

Stop... Before you close this book, get your free bonus...

Scan Above to Claim Bonus

Or Go To: http://bit.ly/1NKyFuQ

101 Life Success Tips – Start Accomplishing Your Goals Today!
Steve Williams is a motivational expert who has helped thousands of people accomplish their dreams and goals. Here are a few tips he has learned along the way to improving success in his life quickly.

----

1. **Use Visualization.** Visualize what your life will be like when you accomplish your goals. If you cannot see yourself accomplishing your goals, then chances are, you will not accomplish them. Remember that you are to keep your eye on the prize at the end of the road. There will be times when you feel as if you are stuck and that you are not making any progress toward your goal, but what you need to do when

this happens is to remember what your life will be like in 6 months or a year if you continue to work toward your goals. Spend a few minutes with your eyes closed, visualizing how great you will feel and all of the changes that will take place in your life once you reach these goals.

2. **Read Books, a Lot of Books**. For each of these tips, there is a book out there that will give you deeper insight into each tip. Spend time reading each and every day. This will not only exercise your brain and help you learn, but it will also help to relieve the stress you have to deal with on a daily basis. Even if you are not reading a book about self-improvement, make sure you take some time each day to read. Reading fiction books helps to release the creativity we have within ourselves, which can help you solve problems down the road.

3. **Accept That You are Responsible for Your Life.** You are in charge of your life, no one else. You cannot blame your failures on your parents or on what happened to you when you were in high school. You need to work through any issues you may have but while doing so, understand that no one makes your life what it is except you. If you are not succeeding in life, no one has caused this except for you and when you are successful, you will have no one to thank for it but yourself.

4. **Learn How to Accept Failure and *Learn from It***. Failure, it is something that all of us will face at one point in our lives, no matter what we do to avoid it. You have two choices when it comes to failure. You can either allow the failure to upset you and stop you in your tracks, or you can learn from the failure and change what you do in the future. One example of this may be that you are trying to

lose weight, you are tempted by a chocolate cake, and end up eating all of it. Now you have failed. You can either choose to give up on your weight loss goals and eat lots of chocolate cake in the following days, which will most likely cause you to gain more weight, or you can learn from your mistake, understand that you lack the will power to stop eating after a small piece of chocolate cake, avoid it in the future, and move on with your diet and weight loss plan.

5. **Do the Things You Dread the Most First.** No matter what it is that you want to do, you should always do the things that you dread the most first. This is called eating the frog. This way you are not putting these tasks off while finishing up more enjoyable tasks, you simply do them, get them out of the way, and then you can move on to the tasks you will enjoy more.

This is a brand new report that will show you 101 quick ways to improve your life success. These are just a sample. You can have the entire report <u>for free.</u>

Steve Williams

The Successful Coach

Check Out My Other Books

Below, you'll find some of my other popular books on Amazon and Kindle. Simply scan the link below to visit my author page on Amazon to see my works.

Direct Link - http://www.amazon.com/Steve-Williams/e/B0125EAWUQ/

The Winning Resume – Get Hired Today With These Groundbreaking Resume Secrets

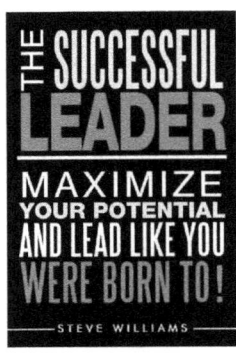

The Successful Leader – Maximize Your Potential And Lead Like You Were Born To!

The Successful Interview – 7 Secrets You Didn't Know About Landing Your Dream Job

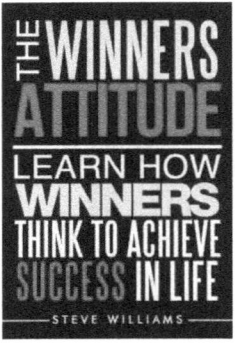

The Winners Attitude – Learn How Winners Think to Achieve Success in Life

Quit Smoking Today! The Most Painless Ways to Permanently Stop Smoking

101 Life Success Tips – Start Accomplishing Your Goals Today!

If the links do not work, for whatever reason, you can simply search for these titles on the Amazon website to find them.

www.ingramcontent.com/pod-product-compliance
Lightning Source LLC
Chambersburg PA
CBHW071415040426
42444CB00009B/2267